THE KINGFISHER
First Dinosaur Picture Atlas

Written by David Burnie

Illustrated by Anthony Lewis

KINGFISHER
NEW YORK

Copyright © 2007 by Macmillan Children's Books
KINGFISHER
Published in the United States by Kingfisher, an imprint
of Henry Holt and Company LLC, 175 Fifth Avenue, New
York, New York 10010. First published in Great Britain
by Kingfisher Publications plc, an imprint of Macmillan
Children's Books, London.

Distributed in Canada by H. B. Fenn and Company Ltd.

Library of Congress Cataloging-in-Publication-Data
Burnie, David.
  First dinosaur picture atlas / David Burnie.—1st ed.
     p. cm.
  Includes index.
  ISBN 978-0-7534-6093-1
  1. Dinosaurs—Juvenile literature. 2. Dinosaurs—
Geographical distribution—Juvenile literature. 3. Dinosaurs—
Maps—Juvenile literature.
  I. Title.
  QE861.5.B875 2008
  567.9—dc22
                                          2007031019

ISBN: 978-0-7534-6093-1

Kingfisher books are available for special promotions and
premiums. For details contact: Director of Special Markets,
Holtzbrinck Publishers.

First American Edition June 2008
Printed in Taiwan
10 9 8 7 6 5 4 3 2 1
1TR/0208/SHENS/SC(SC)/128MS/C

MAP KEY

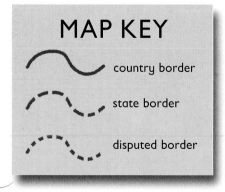

country border

state border

disputed border

Contents

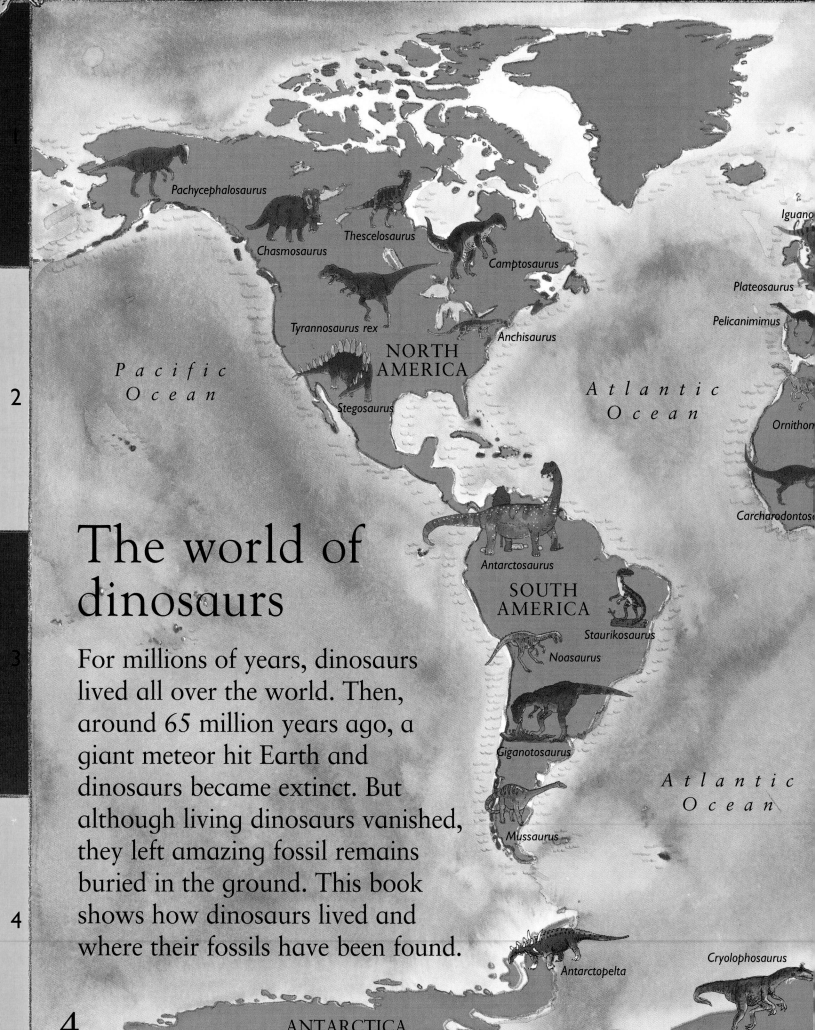

The world of dinosaurs

For millions of years, dinosaurs lived all over the world. Then, around 65 million years ago, a giant meteor hit Earth and dinosaurs became extinct. But although living dinosaurs vanished, they left amazing fossil remains buried in the ground. This book shows how dinosaurs lived and where their fossils have been found.

Pachycephalosaurus

Chasmosaurus

Thescelosaurus

Camptosaurus

Tyrannosaurus rex

Anchisaurus

NORTH AMERICA

Pacific Ocean

Stegosaurus

Atlantic Ocean

Iguano

Plateosaurus

Pelicanimimus

Ornithom

Carcharodontos

Antarctosaurus

SOUTH AMERICA

Staurikosaurus

Noasaurus

Giganotosaurus

Atlantic Ocean

Mussaurus

Antarctopelta

Cryolophosaurus

4

ANTARCTICA

ASIA

EUROPE

ruthiosaurus

Jakartosaurus

Saurolophus

Sinornithosaurus

Tarbosaurus

Fukuisaurus

Spinosaurus

Lufengosaurus

Ouranosaurus

Dravidosaurus

*P a c i f i c
O c e a n*

Allosaurus

AFRICA

Majungatholus

Syntarsus

*I n d i a n
O c e a n*

Muttaburrasaurus

AUSTRALIA

Melanorosaurus

Ozraptor

Rapator

Ankylosaurus

How a fossil is made

A fossil forms when an animal
dies and its remains are
buried. Its bones are
slowly replaced by minerals,
turning them into stone.
Millions of years later, the
fossil may be exposed if the
rock around it is worn away.

Dinosaur dies

Buried body becomes fossilized

Fossil becomes exposed

Age of dinosaurs

Dinosaurs lived on Earth for more than 160 million years. Scientists split this time into three periods: Triassic, Jurassic, and Cretaceous. During each period, many different dinosaurs evolved and died out. Earth's surface also changed as the continents slowly drifted apart into the seven continents that exist today.

Earth in the Cretaceous period

Triassic
Compsognathus

This period started 251 million years ago. At the beginning of the Triassic, most of the world's land was joined in a huge supercontinent called Pangaea.

Dinosaur hunters

The first dinosaur fossils were dug up in Europe in the 1800s. Since then, dinosaur hunters have found fossils on every continent, including Antarctica. The giant fossilized bones being uncovered here in Niger, Africa, are those of a large plant eater.

Jurassic Brachiosaurus

This period started around 200 million years ago. In Jurassic times, Pangaea began to break apart. The continents drifted away from one another, taking the animals with them.

Cretaceous Tyrannosaurus rex

This period began 145 million years ago. It ended 65 million years ago when a huge meteor struck Earth, wiping out the dinosaurs.

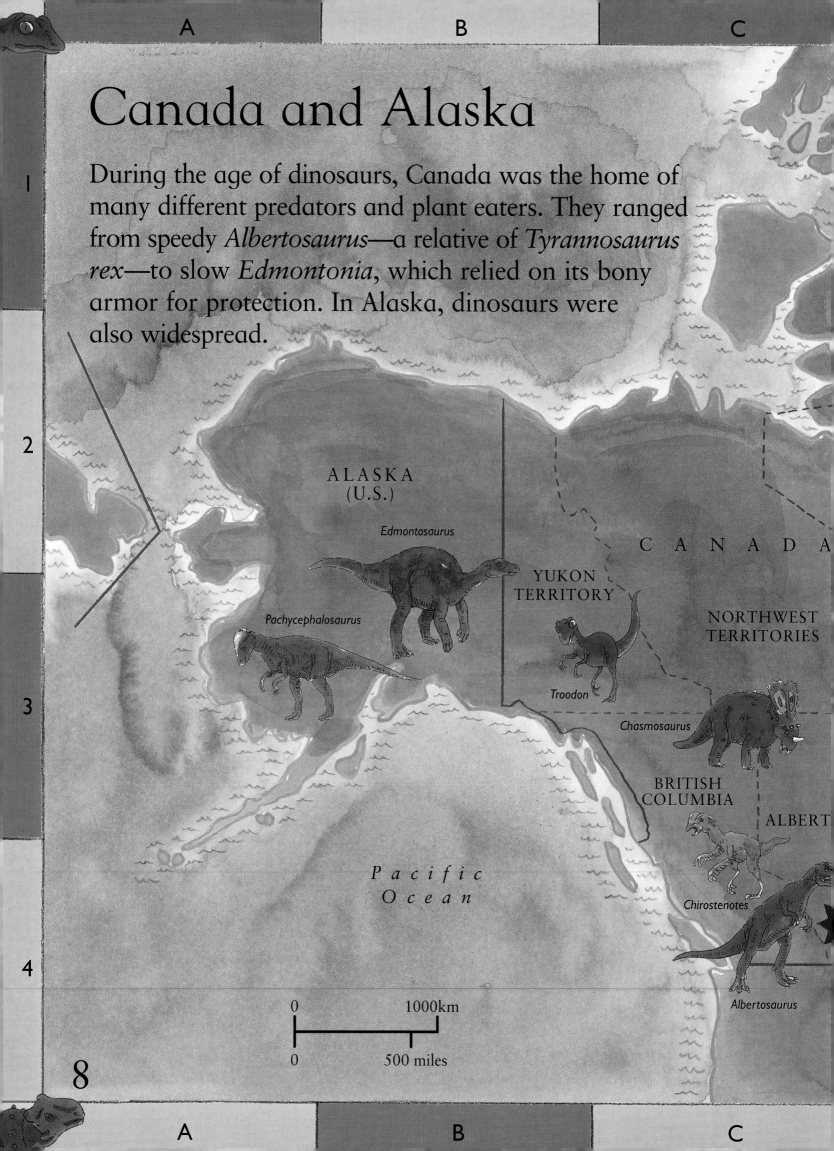

Canada and Alaska

During the age of dinosaurs, Canada was the home of many different predators and plant eaters. They ranged from speedy *Albertosaurus*—a relative of *Tyrannosaurus rex*—to slow *Edmontonia*, which relied on its bony armor for protection. In Alaska, dinosaurs were also widespread.

1

2

3

4

ALASKA
(U.S.)

Edmontosaurus

Pachycephalosaurus

YUKON
TERRITORY

Troodon

C A N A D A

NORTHWEST
TERRITORIES

Chasmosaurus

BRITISH
COLUMBIA

ALBERT

Chirostenotes

P a c i f i c
O c e a n

Albertosaurus

0   1000km

0   500 miles

Dinosaur park

Canada has one of the world's most famous dinosaur graveyards—Dinosaur Provincial Park in southern Alberta. There, almost 40 types of dinosaurs have been found, dating back more than 75 million years.

Look for the star

NUNAVUT

Euoplocephalus

MANITOBA

Thescelosaurus

trosaurus

Edmontonia

Lambeosaurus

SASKATCHEWAN

ONTARIO

QUÉBEC

Atlantic Ocean

NEWFOUNDLAND AND LABRADOR

NEW BRUNSWICK

PRINCE EDWARD ISLAND

NOVA SCOTIA

9

Pack attack

In the age of dinosaurs, Canada was a much warmer place than it is today. It was covered by lush plants—making it a perfect feeding ground for *Lambeosaurus*, a duck-billed dinosaur with a large hollow crest on its head. *Lambeosaurus* had many enemies, including dromaeosaurs, which hunted and attacked in groups.

Toothless wonder
Chirostenotes had a bony crest on its head and beak-shaped jaws without any teeth. It hunted smaller animals, pecking at them just like today's birds.

Lambeosaurus

Dromaeosaurus

Just for show

Chasmosaurus had a giant frill behind its head. Instead of being solid, the frill had a bony framework covered with skin. It might have been used to frighten off rivals or attract mates.

Night shift

Troodon had unusually large eyes, which may have helped it hunt at night. It probably chased small mammals that came out to feed when other dinosaurs were asleep.

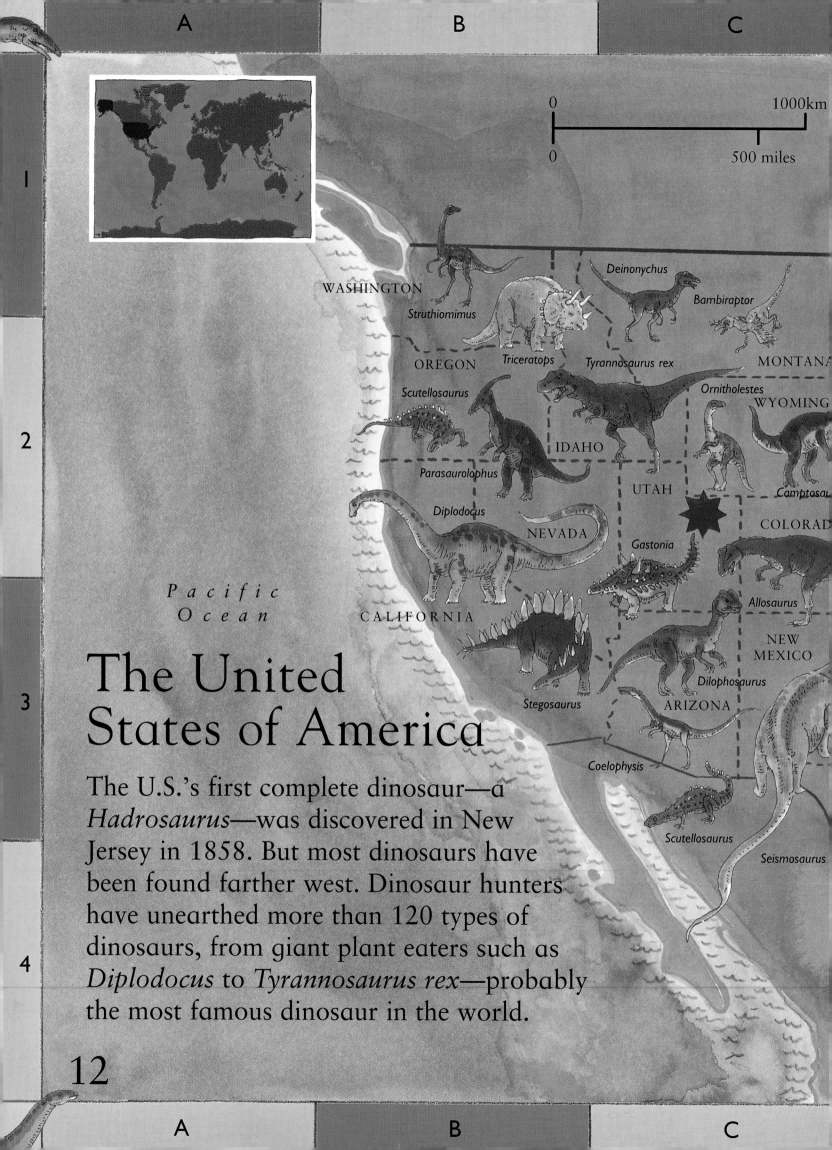

1000km

0

0

500 miles

1

2

3

4

WASHINGTON

Struthiomimus

OREGON

Scutellosaurus

Parasaurolophus

Diplodocus

NEVADA

Deinonychus

Triceratops

Tyrannosaurus rex

IDAHO

UTAH

Gastonia

CALIFORNIA

Bambiraptor

MONTANA

Ornitholestes

WYOMING

Camptosa

COLORAD

Allosaurus

*Pacific
Ocean*

Stegosaurus

ARIZONA

Coelophysis

NEW
MEXICO

Dilophosaurus

Scutellosaurus

Seismosaurus

The United
States of America

The U.S.'s first complete dinosaur—a
Hadrosaurus—was discovered in New
Jersey in 1858. But most dinosaurs have
been found farther west. Dinosaur hunters
have unearthed more than 120 types of
dinosaurs, from giant plant eaters such as
Diplodocus to *Tyrannosaurus rex*—probably
the most famous dinosaur in the world.

Bone bed

The "dinosaur wall" at Dinosaur National Monument in Utah contains hundreds of dinosaur fossils on a ledge of sloping rock. This man is clearing rock, leaving the bones as they were found.

Look for the star

Maiasaura

Ceratosaurus

Apatosaurus

Stegoceras

Coelophysis

Anchisaurus

Hadrosaurus

MINNESOTA

MICHIGAN

MAINE

VERMONT

NEW HAMPSHIRE

NEW YORK

MASSACHUSETTS

RHODE ISLAND

CONNECTICUT

NEW JERSEY

WISCONSIN

IOWA

PENNSYLVANIA

OHIO

DELAWARE

ILLINOIS

INDIANA

WEST VIRGINIA

MARYLAND

KANSAS

MISSOURI

KENTUCKY

VIRGINIA

TENNESSEE

NORTH CAROLINA

OKLAHOMA

ARKANSAS

MISSISSIPPI

SOUTH CAROLINA

TEXAS

ALABAMA

GEORGIA

LOUISIANA

FLORIDA

Atlantic Ocean

Gulf of Mexico

RTH OTA

OUTH KOTA

ASKA

13

Dinosaur nest in Montana

In the 1970s, dinosaur hunters made an incredible find in the mountains of Montana. As well as many fossilized dinosaur bones, they found nests, eggs, and baby dinosaurs. The nests belonged to *Maiasaura*, or "good mother lizard." This plant-eating dinosaur laid up to 40 eggs in a mound-shaped nest and brought food to its young.

Maiasaura

14

Protoceratops fossilized eggs

Dinosaur eggs

Like reptiles today, most dinosaurs laid eggs. Compared to their size, dinosaur eggs were often quite small. Some were round, and others were long and narrow. These eggs were laid by **Protoceratops**, a dinosaur that lived in Mongolia (north-central Asia).

Growing up

When newly hatched, **Maiasaura** had a tiny skull and teeth that were smaller than a two-year-old child's. As it grew, its skull became bigger and longer, giving it a strong bite for crushing plants.

hatchling Maiasaura skull

adult Maiasaura skull

North American dinosaurs

Triceratops looked fierce, but it was actually a plant eater. It was up to four times as heavy as a rhinoceros, and its horns could be as much as three feet long. It used its horns to fight back against strong predators such as *Tyrannosaurus rex*.

Tyrannosaurus rex

Triceratops

King of the dinosaurs

Tyrannosaurus rex was one of the biggest two-legged predators, and it lived at the end of the age of dinosaurs. It ambushed smaller dinosaurs, but it also scavenged on the dead remains of other dinosaurs.

Tyrannosaurus rex

Scutellosaurus

Danger in numbers

Slim, lightweight, and fast-moving, **Deinonychus** hunted in a pack. This dinosaur was able to catch and kill larger dinosaurs that moved too slowly to escape.

Tenontosaurus

Deinonychus

Deadly swing

Ankylosaurus had armored skin and a tail club that weighed up to 110 pounds. By swinging its club, it could smash open the skull of a large predator.

17

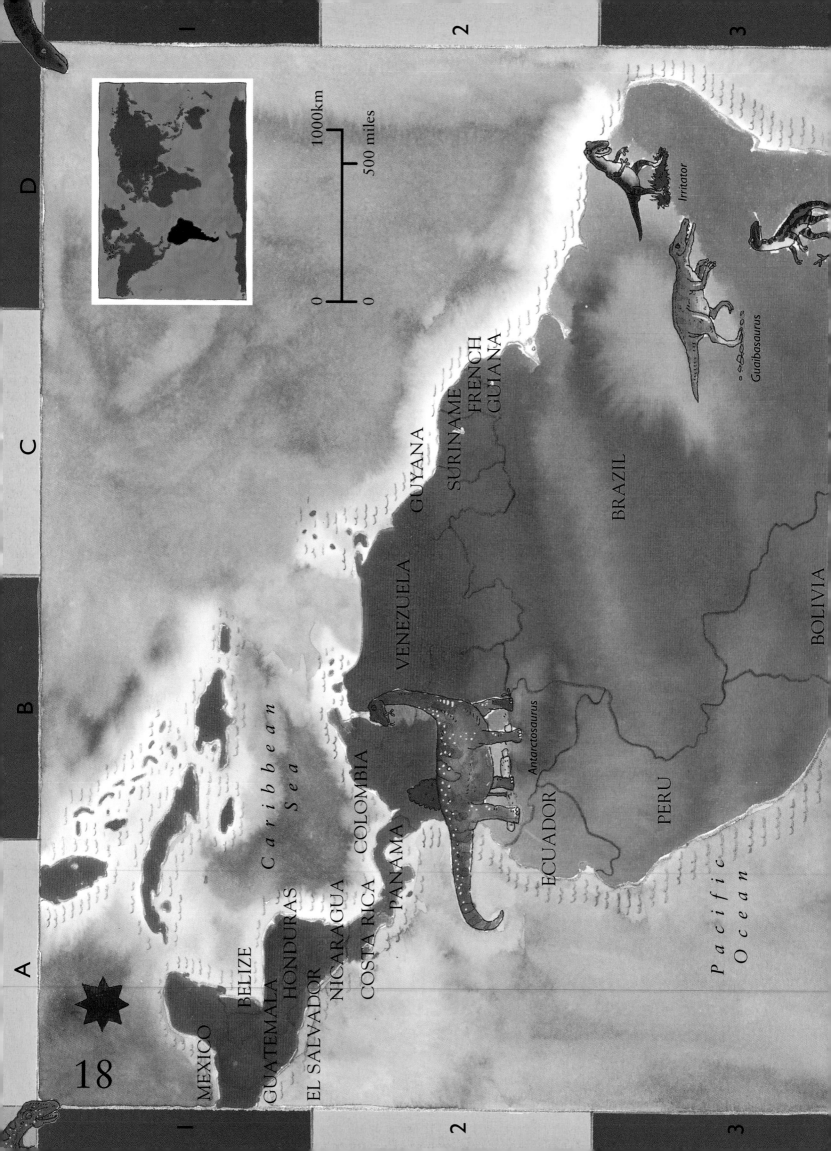

MEXICO

BELIZE

GUATEMALA

HONDURAS

EL SALVADOR

NICARAGUA

COSTA RICA

PANAMA

COLOMBIA

VENEZUELA

GUYANA

SURINAME

FRENCH GUIANA

ECUADOR

PERU

BRAZIL

BOLIVIA

Caribbean Sea

Pacific Ocean

Antarctosaurus

Guaibasaurus

Irritator

1000km

500 miles

0

0

A B C D

1

2

3

Central and South America

Some of the world's earliest and biggest dinosaurs have been discovered in South America. These include *Eoraptor*, a chicken-size dinosaur that lived more than 225 million years ago, and *Saltasaurus*, a colossal plant eater that may have weighed almost 100 tons.

PARAGUAY

URUGUAY

ARGENTINA

CHILE

Saltasaurus

Herrerasaurus

Giganotosaurus

Noasaurus

Carnotaurus

Eoraptor

Argentinosaurus

Abelisaurus

Piatnitzkysaurus

Mussaurus

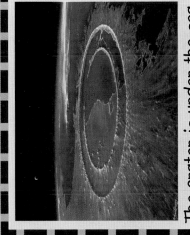

The crater is under the sea.

Experts think that dinosaurs died out after a giant meteor crashed into Earth 65 million years ago. A huge crater has been found in the sea off the coast of Mexico, showing where the meteor might have struck.

Look for the star

Dinosaur hunters in Argentina

In Argentina's Valley of the Moon, scientists have found fossils of some of the earliest dinosaurs. One of them, *Herrerasaurus*, lived 228 million years ago. It was 20 feet long and hunted by running on its back legs.

fossilized skeleton of a Piatnitzkysaur

Out of reach

Like many hunting dinosaurs, **Piatnitzkysaurus** had huge back legs but tiny arms. It also had only three fingers on each of its hands.

Handy work

Eoraptor is another very early dinosaur that lived in the Valley of the Moon. Small and quick, it probably ate small animals as well as plants. It could hold the food it caught in its five-fingered hands.

Going to extremes

Giganotosaurus lived more than 100 million years after **Herrerasaurus** and **Eoraptor**. It was one of the biggest hunting dinosaurs, weighing as much as seven tons.

Eoraptor

Herrerasaurus

21

South American dinosaurs

Carnotaurus was one of the strangest dinosaurs from South America. Its skin was covered with knobby scales, and it had a small head, with a horn above each eye. It might have used the horns like bulls do when they fight rivals to win the right to mate with a female. The name *Carnotaurus* means "meat-eating bull."

fossilized skeleton of a baby Mussaurus

Tiny dino

The smallest complete dinosaur fossil is a baby **Mussaurus** from Argentina. It measures only seven inches long. **Mussaurus** fed on plants. When fully grown, it probably grew to 16 feet.

Carnotaurus

Tipping the scales

Saltasaurus was a plant eater that lived in Argentina. Its back was covered with hard bony plates, like those that protect today's crocodiles.

Slashing claw

Noasaurus might have had slashing claws on its hands. Measuring only eight feet from head to tail, it would have been light enough to be able to leap on its prey.

23

Europe

In Europe, dinosaur fossils have been studied since the early 1800s, when naturalists figured out that they belonged to giant extinct reptiles. Since then, a huge variety of fossils have been found, including giant plant eaters such as *Brachiosaurus* and also *Baryonyx*—one of the few dinosaurs that ate mostly fish.

Early bird

Europe's fossils include many other prehistoric animals besides dinosaurs. The world's earliest known bird, called **Archaeopteryx**, was discovered in a limestone quarry in southern Germany. Around the size of a crow, it had teeth and a long, bony tail. However, it also had feathers and could fly.

Can you find Archaeopteryx?

fossilized skeleton of an Archaeopteryx

North Sea

SCOTLAND

Saltasaurus

UNITED KINGDOM

Megalosaurus

NORTHERN IRELAND

Eustreptospondylus

IRELAND

Dinosaur herd in Belgium

In 1878, a team of Belgian miners found 38 *Iguanodon* skeletons—the remains of a herd that lived more than 120 million years ago. The dinosaurs might have died when they tried to escape from predators, falling into a deep ravine.

fossilized Iguanodon skeletons

Fossil herd

These skeletons of a Belgian **Iguanodon** herd are kept together in a museum. It is the largest display of a single type of dinosaur anywhere in the world.

measuring fossilized
dinosaur tracks

gingko

conifer

cycad

fern

horsetail

Lasting imprint

Like other dinosaurs, **Iguanodon** often left tracks where it walked in soft mud. Fossilized tracks show that adult **Iguanodons** usually walked on all fours.

Vegetarian diet

Iguanodon fed only on plants. It ate ferns, horsetails, and many other types of plants, but not grasses—this did not exist when **Iguanodon** was alive.

European dinosaurs

Most dinosaurs fed on land, but *Baryonyx* was different. It had jaws like a crocodile's and long claws, especially on its thumbs. It probably waded into the shallows of rivers and lakes and caught fish as they swam past. One fossil of *Baryonyx* from southern England has fish bones and scales inside it.

Baryonyx

Feeding in the treetops

Brachiosaurus was up to 82 feet long, and its cranelike neck could reach almost twice as high as a giraffe's. It fed on leaves, tearing them off with its peg-shaped teeth. This sauropod lived in Europe, North America, and Africa.

Little grinder

One of the smallest plant-eating dinosaurs, **Hypsilophodon** had a head the size of an adult human's hand. It fed on low-growing plants, grinding them up with its ridged teeth. It lived in herds and relied on its speed and sharp senses to escape danger, just like deer do today.

fossil of a
Hypsilophodon skull

Chasing lizards

Compsognathus was a small, speedy dinosaur with a chicken-size body and a long neck and tail. It fed on lizards and other small animals, tearing them apart with its claws and teeth.

29

D   C   B   A

1

2

3

500 miles

1000km

0   0

MOROCCO

ALGERIA | TUNISIA

WESTERN
SAHARA

MAURITANIA

MALI

SENEGAL

GUINEA

SIERRA
LEONE

LIBERIA

IVORY
COAST

BURKINA
FASO

GHANA

TOGO

BENIN

NIGER

NIGERIA

LIBYA

CHAD

EGYPT

SUDAN

ERITREA

ETHIOPIA

SOMALIA

CENTRAL
AFRICAN
REPUBLIC

CAMEROON

GABON

CONGO

DEMOCRATIC
REPUBLIC OF
THE CONGO

UGANDA

KENYA

TANZANIA

SÃO TOMÉ AND PRÍNCIPE

Spinosaurus

Ornithomimus

Brachiosaurus

Suchomimus

Carcharodontosaurus

Afrovenator

Ouranosaurus

Allosaurus

Kentrosaurus

30

Africa

Throughout Africa dinosaur hunters have found fascinating fossils. They include some of the oldest dinosaurs, as well as the tallest and the most fearsome. *Spinosaurus* weighed almost twice as much as an African elephant, while *Brachiosaurus* towered over smaller plant-eating dinosaurs as it browsed the tops of trees.

Changing climate

In the Sahara Desert, dinosaur hunters uncover the fossilized remains of **Afrovenator**, a giant predator found in Niger in 1993. When the dinosaur was alive, the Sahara was damp and lush, with plenty of plant-eating prey.

Can you find Afrovenator?

ANGOLA

ZAMBIA

NAMIBIA

MOZAMBIQUE

MADAGASCAR

SOUTH AFRICA

Ceratosaurus

Majungatholus

Vulcanodon

Syntarsus

Melanorosaurus

Lesothosaurus

Heterodontosaurus

Massospondylus

Euskelosaurus

1 THE GAMBIA
2 GUINEA-BISSAU
3 EQUATORIAL GUINEA
4 DJIBOUTI
5 RWANDA
6 BURUNDI
7 MALAWI
8 ZIMBABWE
9 BOTSWANA
10 SWAZILAND
11 LESOTHO

31

A B C D

Duel in Tanzania

In east Africa, a hungry *Ceratosaurus* tries to attack *Kentrosaurus*, a slow-moving plant eater. *Kentrosaurus* is smaller but is protected by bony plates and spikes that are up to 23 inches long. Each time the predator moves in, *Kentrosaurus* swivels around and lashes out with its tail.

Ceratosaurus

Kentrosaurus

Big is best

Brachiosaurus relied on its size to stay out of danger. This enormous plant eater might have weighed up to 80 tons—much more than the biggest predators of its time. But when this giant got old and weak, it was easy prey to a **Ceratosaurus**.

Brachiosaurus

Ceratosaurus

fossilized skeleton of a Kentrosaurus

Bundle of nerves

Kentrosaurus had a small head and a tiny brain. Above its hips, it had a nerve center, or "second brain," that controlled its back legs and spike-studded tail.

Run for your life

At only 3.9 feet high, **Heterodontosaurus** had no hope of fighting **Ceratosaurus**. Instead, this lightweight dinosaur sprinted away at the first sign of trouble.

Ceratosaurus

Heterodontosaurus

33

African dinosaurs

Spinosaurus was one of the largest predatory dinosaurs, weighing as much as nine tons. In addition to having fearsome teeth and powerful jaws, it had a six-foot-high "sail." It might have used the sail like a solar panel, soaking up warmth at sunrise and sunset.

Spinosaurus

Quick exit

Massopondylus lived around 190 million years ago, toward the beginning of the age of dinosaurs. It ate mostly plants and was lightweight. If danger threatened, it sped away on its back legs.

fossilized skull of a Carcharadontosaurus

Giant bite

For pure biting power, few dinosaurs could match **Carcharadontosaurus**. Its skull was five feet long. Its teeth had serrated edges—the biggest teeth were almost as long as a human skull.

Clever hunter

In 1993, researchers found the skeleton of an unknown dinosaur in the Sahara Desert. Although it was 125 million years old, the fossil was almost complete. Called **Afrovenator**—"African hunter"— it was around 30 feet long. It might have hunted fish in shallow water.

1

2

3

4

Jaxartosaurus

Psittacosaurus

MONGOLIA

Velociraptor

Saurolophus

Aralosaurus

KAZAKHSTAN

Protoceratop

Alioramus

Homalocephe

UZBEKISTAN

KYRGYZSTAN

Shantungosaurus

TURKMENISTAN

TAJIKISTAN

Pinacosaurus

Gallimimus

Mamenchisaurus

AFGHANISTAN

Shunosaurus

Tuojiangosaurus

PAKISTAN

IRAN

NEPAL

Lufengosaur

C H I N A

Barapasaurus

INDIA

BHUTAN

VIETNAM

Isisaurus

BANGLADESH

Indosuchus

MYANMAR
(BURMA)

LAOS

*Arabian
Sea*

Kotasaurus

*Bay of
Bengal*

THAILAND

CAMBOI

36

Dravidosaurus

SRI LANKA

RUSSIA

0   1000km

0   500 miles

Therizinosaurus

Nemegtosaurus

Microraptor

Sinornithosaurus

Oviraptor

Caudipteryx

Beipiaosaurus

NORTH KOREA

SOUTH KOREA

Tarbosaurus

Tsintaosaurus

JAPAN

Fukuisaurus

Fukuiraptor

Pacific Ocean

Bone dry

Central Asia's desert climate is perfect for preserving fossils. Here, a scientist is preparing the skull of a **Protoceratops** so that it can be removed without breaking apart.

Can you find Protoceratops?

Asia

The dry and windswept deserts of central Asia have yielded a spectacular amount of dinosaur fossils. At Mongolia's Flaming Cliffs, dinosaur hunters have found beaked plant eaters such as *Protoceratops*, swift hunters such as *Velociraptor*, and amazing collections of dinosaur eggs. Farther east, in China, feathered dinosaurs show how birds evolved.

37

Asian dinosaurs

Most of today's reptiles don't make any noise, but dinosaurs were very different. *Saurolophus*, from Asia and North America, made calls by inflating a pouch of skin that was above its snout. These calls would have filled the air when an entire *Saurolophus* herd spotted danger heading its way.

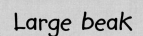

Large beak

Psittacosaurus, a plant eater, had a beak like a parrot's. It stood just over three feet high at the shoulder but was able to reach taller plants by standing on its back legs.

Tarbosaurus

Saurolophus

scientist examining arms of
Deinocheirus fossil

Scary claws

In the late 1960s, researchers in
Mongolia found a huge pair of arm
bones ending in ten-inch-long claws.
Very few other bones of their owner,
Deinocheirus, have been found.

Nest raider

Gallimimus fed on the eggs and
young of other dinosaurs, using its
arms to dig and pick up food.
Its long neck helped it spot food
that was far away.

Dinosaur fight in Mongolia

Velociraptor and *Protoceratops* were deadly enemies. One fossil, found in the Gobi Desert, shows them locked in combat. *Velociraptor* was attacking with its claws, while *Protoceratops* hit back with its beak. They died suddenly, probably because they were smothered by a sandstorm or buried by a collapsing dune.

Protoceratops

Velociraptor

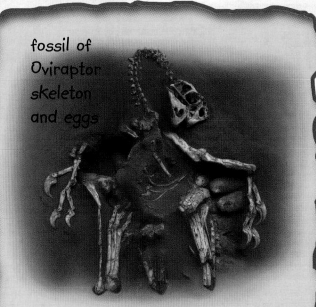

fossil of
Oviraptor
skeleton
and eggs

Mother love

Some dinosaurs were very protective
parents. This fossil is of an adult
Oviraptor that died while sitting on
its eggs. Inside each egg there are
the tiny bones of the babies.

Low blows

The plant eater **Pinacosaurus** fought
its enemies using a club on the end
of its tail. By swinging the club close
to the ground, it could smash
a predator's legs, knocking it
off its feet. Bony armor also
helped keep it out of trouble.

Head-to-head collision

Homalocephale had an extrathick layer of bone on
the top of its skull. The males might have used this
in head-butting contests, fighting to attract mates.

Feathered dinosaurs of China

In Liaoning, in eastern China, researchers
have found dinosaurs with fuzzy outlines of
feathers instead of scaly skin. Some—including
Caudipteryx—had feathers to stay warm. Others
had bigger feathers and used them to fly. Scientists
are certain that birds evolved from dinosaurs.

Caudipteryx

Pointed scale

Fluffy feather

Feather with vanes

From scales to feathers
Feathers evolved gradually from hard, pointed scales. Fluffy feathers evolved first, helping keep dinosaurs warm. From these came much bigger feathers with branched vanes—the type that were inherited by the world's first true birds.

Ground attack
Protarchaeopteryx had long feathers on its arms, but it could not fly. It probably used its feathers like a scoop to catch insects and other small animals.

Winged flier
Microraptor was one of the smallest dinosaurs. It had feathers on its legs and arms, and it probably used all four limbs to fly. Instead of taking off from the ground, it might have jumped from trees.

Australia and New Zealand

Not many dinosaurs have been found in Australia. This is partly because most of Australia was covered by the ocean for most of the age of dinosaurs. Even so, Australia was the home of unusual dinosaurs, including the giant sauropod *Austrosaurus* and *Minmi*, an armored dinosaur covered with bony plates.

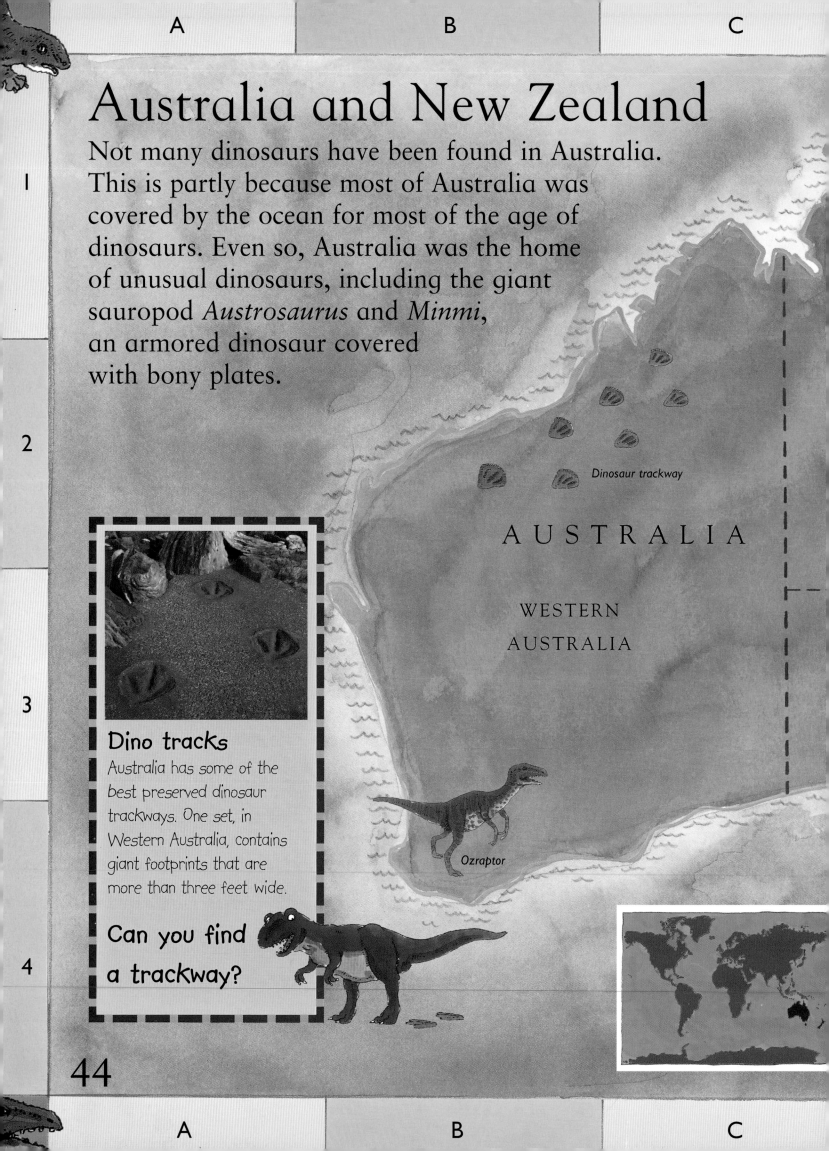

Dinosaur trackway

A U S T R A L I A

WESTERN
AUSTRALIA

Ozraptor

Dino tracks

Australia has some of the best preserved dinosaur trackways. One set, in Western Australia, contains giant footprints that are more than three feet wide.

Can you find a trackway?

44

0
1000km

0
500 miles

NORTH
ISLAND

Ankylosaurus

NEW
ZEALAND

NORTHERN
TERRITORY

Muttaburrasaurus

Austrosaurus

Minmi

QUEENSLAND

SOUTH
AUSTRALIA

Rhoetosaurus

Kakuru

NEW
SOUTH
WALES

Rapator

Qantassaurus

Timimus

Atlascopcosaurus

Leaellynasaura

VICTORIA

1

2

3

4

45

Glossary

ambush
To attack by surprise.

armored dinosaur
A plant-eating dinosaur protected by tough scales or bony plates.

continent
One of Earth's seven huge areas of land. In the age of dinosaurs, the continents were in different positions than they are today.

crater
A deep hollow made by a volcano or by a meteor hitting Earth.

crest
A large flap on top of a dinosaur's head.

Cretaceous period
The last part of the age of dinosaurs, which ended suddenly when a meteor struck Earth.

dinosaur hunter
Someone who searches for dinosaur fossils and digs them up.

duck-billed dinosaur
A dinosaur with a mouth like a beak and no front teeth. Also known as a hadrosaur.

evolve
To change gradually over thousands or millions of years. As living things evolve, new types gradually appear, while older ones slowly become extinct, or die out.

extinct
No longer living anywhere on Earth. Dinosaurs are now extinct, in addition to many other giant reptiles.

fossil
Hard parts of an animal's body that slowly have changed to stone deep in the ground.

herd
A group of animals that live, feed, and breed together.

horn
A hard body part with a sharp point, usually found on a dinosaur's head.

insect
A small animal with six legs such as a beetle or a bee. The first insects appeared long before the first dinosaurs.

Jurassic period
The middle part of the age of dinosaurs.

limb
A front or back arm or leg.

limestone
A type of layered rock that often contains fossils.

mammal
A warm-blooded animal that feeds its babies milk.

meteor
A piece of rock that has reached Earth from space.

naturalist
Someone who studies animals and plants.

nerves
Parts of the body that work like wiring, helping an animal feel and move.

Pangaea
A huge supercontinent that existed at the beginning of the age of dinosaurs.

predator
An animal that hunts other animals for its food.

prehistoric
Anything that lived in the distant past, long before human history began.

prey
An animal that is hunted and eaten by other animals.

quarry
A place where rock is dug up so that it can be used. Quarries are often good places for finding fossil

reptile
A cold-blooded animal with scaly skin that usually breeds by laying eggs. Dinosaurs were the biggest reptiles that ever lived.

sauropod
A huge, long-necked dinosaur that fed on plants. The largest dinosaurs were all sauropods.

scales
Small, hard plates that cover a reptile's skin.

scavenging
Feeding on the remains of dead animals.

serrated
Having jagged edges.

trackway
A place where dinosaurs often walked, leaving fossilized footprint

Triassic period
The first part of the age of dinosaurs.

ndex

Photographic acknowledgments

The Publisher would like to thank the following for permission to reproduce their material. Every care has
been taken to trace copyright holders. However, if there have been unintentional omissions or failure to trace
copyright holders, we apologize and will, if informed, endeavor to make corrections in any future edition.

Pages: 5 Natural History Museum, London; 9 Jonathan Blair/Corbis; 13 James L. Amos/Corbis;
15 Natural History Museum, London; 19 D. van Ravenswaay/Science Photo Library; 20 Kevin Schafer/Corbis;
24 Sally A. Morgan/Corbis; 26l Museum of Natural Science, Belgium; 26r Ian West; 29 Natural History
Museum; 31 Didier Dutheil/Corbis; 33 DK Images; 35 University of Chicago; 37 Louie Psihoyos/Corbis;
39 Louie Psihoyos/Corbis; 41 Louie Psihoyos/Corbis; 44 CWB